That Patchwork Place™

B-72

Cathedral Window -

a

New View

by Mary Ryder Kline

9-22-11

CATHEDRAL WINDOW ©

© Mary Ryder Kline, 1983

0-943574-20-X

3

Dedicated to my Family

Acknowledgments

Many thanks to:

Liz Hensgen and Mary Blaylock, two teachers in Santa Barbara, for giving me encouragement and opportunities to teach their classes;

Marsha McCloskey, author of Small Quilts and Wall Quilts *for paving the way to That Patchwork Place;*

Nancy Martin, President of That Patchwork Place, for being so immediately receptive to my ideas and their development.

The staff of That Patchwork Place for all the valuable work behind the scenes.

Credits:

Photography . . . .*Carl Murray*
Illustration and Graphics . . . .*Mary Ryder Kline*
Stephanie Benson

All items made by the author unless otherwise indicated.

Contents

Introduction

Cathedral Window has always been an orphan among quilt patterns. With the publication of this booklet, three relatives join with Cathedral Window to form a family of patterns. They are Cathedral Spire, Cathedral Gothic and Cathedral Arcade.

Patterns are included for each of the projects pictured with the exception of those items that are made from the traditional Cathedral Window pattern using a square. For Cathedral Spire, the closest relative of Cathedral Window, three patterns of differing sizes are included. Two sizes are offered for Cathedral Gothic and one for Cathedral Arcade.

The smaller projects require only a few completed units and a few spare hours. Two pattern pieces sewn together can be made into a sachet, pin cushion or potholder. Another pattern with only nine background pieces creates a wallhanging. Cathedral Gothic and Cathedral Arcade will each make handsome center medallions on a quilt, pillow or wallhanging.

A complete section on drafting the new Cathedral patterns is offered as a reference tool for designers and teachers.

Cathedral patterns are not for quick quilts. Choose a pattern for the challenge and satisfaction. It is truly easier than it looks. Taken one step at a time, the diagrams and accompanying text will assist in pattern assembly. The grid diagrams illustrate the flexibility of these new patterns and their potential for expansion and original design.

It is not my purpose to lead anyone into a year-long process of making a quilt. That must be an individual decision. But the possibilities for extended, heirloom projects are here. Smaller projects will do well as an introduction to these entirely new designs.

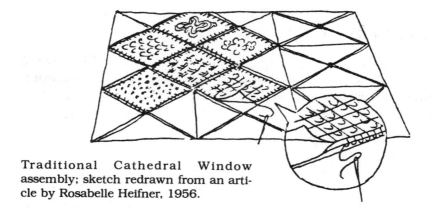

Traditional Cathedral Window assembly; sketch redrawn from an article by Rosabelle Heifner, 1956.

History

The earliest printed instructions to be found to date were in an article that ran in the Iowa Farm and Home Register of June 1956. Accompanying the article was the sketch that is redrawn and printed here. No name was given to the pattern. As you will note, little advantage was taken of the bias edges of fabric that surround the windows.

Quilter's Journal, Winter 1979, carried a rambling account of the earliest known beginnings. They reported that a quilt answering the description of Cathedral Window was seen at the Chicago World's Fair of 1933. Until a little over ten years ago the pattern was known variously as Daisy Block, Mock Orange Blossoms, Attic Window and Pain-in-the-Neck. History can be so unkind!

If indeed the basic design was created by some innovative, patient person in 1933, then Cathedral Window is half a century old this year. In celebration of this 50th anniversary, we present Cathedral Window - A New View.

Construction

The steps of construction are the same for the traditional and the new patterns. Only the shapes have changed.

Pattern	Steps of Assembly		
	1st Stage	2nd Stage	3rd Stage
Traditional Cathedral Window	Square	Square	Square
Cathedral Spire	Polygon	Diamond	Rectangle
Cathedral Gothic	Star	Hexagon	Equilateral Triangle
Cathedral Arcade	Polygon	Polygon	Isosceles Triangle

Marking the center of the pattern is important with all of the designs because the points must be folded to the center at two different stages of assembly. Each time the folds are made, the thickness of the fabric is doubled. This is true of all of the Cathedral patterns and one of the features that make them a related group.

Assembly

Five steps of assembly apply to all of the Cathedral patterns.

(1) Fold points to the center.
(2) Seam together all adjacent edges. Leave small opening in one seam.
(3) Turn right side out. Sew opening shut.
(4) a. Lay flat, seam side up for Cathedral Window and Cathedral Spire.
   b. Lay flat, seam side down for Cathedral Gothic and Cathedral Arcade.
(5) Fold points to the center. Tack points together and through to the back of the unit.

More detailed instructions accompany each pattern.

First Stage Full Pattern	Second Stage Seamed Envelope Double thickness	Third Stage Finished Unit Four Thicknesses

Cathedral
Window

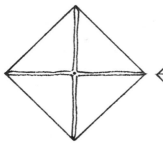

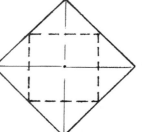

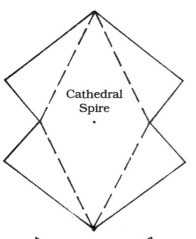

Cathedral
Spire

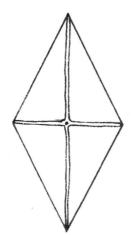

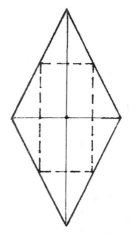

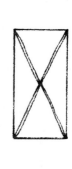

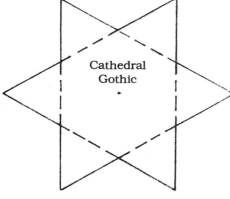

Cathedral
Gothic

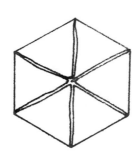

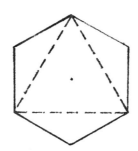

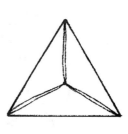

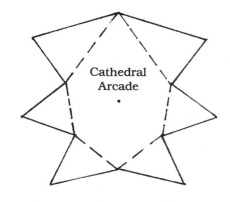

Cathedral
Arcade

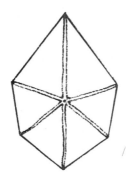

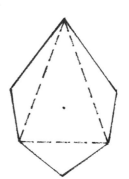

Materials and Machines

By Hand or Machine

The choice is up to you. Hand sewing is emphasized in this booklet. For advocates of the machine, I suggest that you limit your use of it to the beginning steps of assembly, at least until you get a sense of the pattern. I avoid the use of both my machine and my iron, preferring to keep my work completely portable.

The Portable Packet

Keep these six items in a zip-lock bag with a few pattern pieces and you will be ready for a short drive or a long meeting.

(1) Thread
(2) Thimble
(3) Beeswax
(4) Needles, several because they do run away
(5) Scissors, small ones that travel well
(6) Pins, just a few but so essential

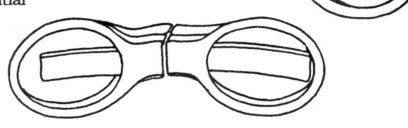

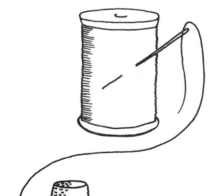

Color in Cathedral Patterns

By all means, use color! Unbleached muslin was, at one time, very reasonable in cost (more so 50 years ago when the first Cathedral Window pattern was designed). Today, it is a good idea to watch for the sales when colors compete with unbleached muslin in price. Dramatic effects are achieved with dark, solid colors in the background grid; however, something of the three-dimensional effect may be lost. Patterned fabric for the grid poses something of the same dilemma. A figured fabric, however muted, is apt to blur the geometric lines and the three-dimensional effect. An exception might be a pin cushion or potholder. These would be handled and seen at close range unlike a hanging or a quilt. You will develop your own preferences. Experimentation is part of the fun. Study the two excellent examples shown on page 29: "Acidita" by Rita Ericson, and "Rose Window" by Janet Kaiser. And remember, if you seek to create contrast, do not overlook one reliable method; work both the background and the windows in contrasting solid colors.

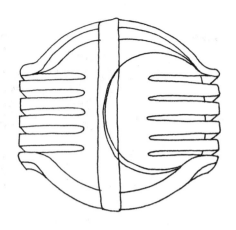

Fabrics

Cotton is recommended for the beginner. You will enjoy working with 100% cotton especially if you use batting. However, one need not be limited to cottons; blends work well. For the windows anything goes (within reason)! Even silks, taffetas and velvets can be used if one is skilled in handling these fabrics.

Batting

It takes only scraps of batting to achieve a good effect. All Cathedral patterns are three-dimensional and the windows are their one most prominent feature. Permit them to bulge with a bit of batting which will give them the prominence they deserve. Any good low-loft polyester batting will do well in Cathedral patterns.

Tools

Many of these are standard items in a sewing basket. A few items on the list are relatively new and take some practice before effective use can be made of them. This is true of the rotary cutter, a marvelous tool when used with a self-healing, cutting board.

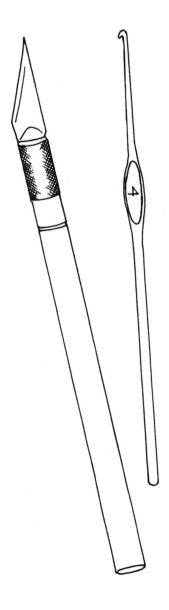

Beeswax

It will strengthen the thread and teach it good manners. Warm the wax on a piece of wax paper in the sunlight and rework it whenever too many deep grooves form in the surface. It lasts forever which is more than can be said for your sweet disposition when the thread tangles.

Compass

A simple one will be useful for drafting patterns.

Crochet Hook

A small one will serve two purposes. One end is good for pulling out a few stitches, the other end is useful for pointing out corners.

Needles and Pins

The choice is up to you. The needles should move easily through the cloth. Pin heads should be small so they do not create an obstacle course.

Paper Cutting Knife

One with removable blades is preferred and, with practice, makes a better paper cutter than scissors.

Paper Weights

The best ones will be found around the house and will work better than pins. Old drapery weights are ideal. So are silver dollars! But smaller change will do. If you are feeling clumsy, get out the cans of tuna!

Pencils

You will need several well sharpened, No. 2 lead pencils. A white quilter's pencil or dressmaker's pencil will take care of marking the fabrics that are too dark for a lead pencil. Water-soluble fabric markers work well for some people. I prefer the thinner line of a lead pencil that does not have to be sponged out.

Rubber Cement or Stick Glue

Either one will do for bonding the paper pattern to the plastic template.

Sandpaper Board

This prevents the fabric from shifting under the template. It is something you can make with one or two large sheets of fine or medium sandpaper. Glue them, without overlapping, to a piece of corrugated cardboard or pressed board. Sandpaper the edge of the pressed board; tape the edge of the cardboard.

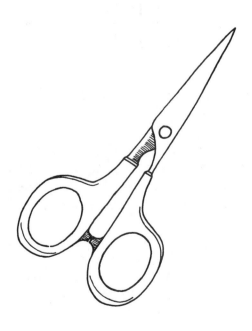

Scissors

Have one for cloth, one for paper and another small pair for snipping.

Seam Ripper

The best planned seams occasionally require ripping.

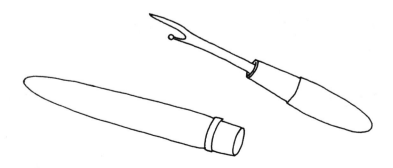

See-Through Plastic Ruler

This is one of the best purchases you can make. Look for the 18" ruler with 1/16" markings in red along the edge.

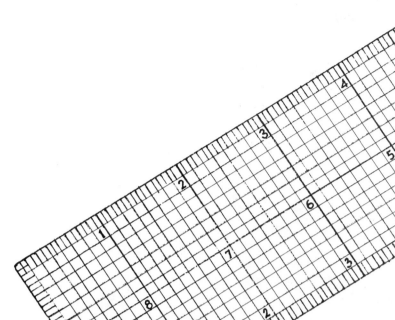

Sheets of Plastic

A good weight for templates can be purchased at art supply stores. Exposed x-ray film and the plastic from some brands of bacon will work as well.

Tape Measure

Any good, non-stretch, dressmaker's tape will do.

Thimble

Yes! You will find it becomes a natural extension of your third finger. If you trim the nail and wet the finger tip, you will find that enough suction is created to keep the thimble from falling off — if it fits in the first place.

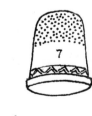

Thread

Always choose a thread to match the grid of the project. Quilting thread is fine for the purist; it is the strongest. When I have to choose strength or color, I always buy the best color and then use my beeswax.

Grid

All Cathedral patterns have a background "grid" and a window "display" area. The grid is inclined to dominate the design, but with a few changes one can expect some exciting results. The grid can be made of several different fabrics and colors to break up the "chain" effect of a single color. Areas of color can be created with windows that blend or match the grid. Experiment with a sheet of tracing paper placed over one of the grids, a few colored pens, and soon you will become the designer.

Shown above is the grid of Cathedral Window. The traditional quilt was made with the grid of unbleached muslin and "sparks" of bright color in the windows.

Shown at the left is the Cathedral Spire grid. These two patterns have the most prominent grids, because the bias is consistently more flexible. The two grids on the adjoining page have more restricted bias, but more dramatic design possibilities as compensation.

Shown on the left is the Cathedral Gothic grid. The pattern of the pillow is defined by the shaded area. Note the position and relationship of the remaining triangles surrounding the star shape of the pillow. These create a series of concentric patterns with room for all colors of the rainbow.

16

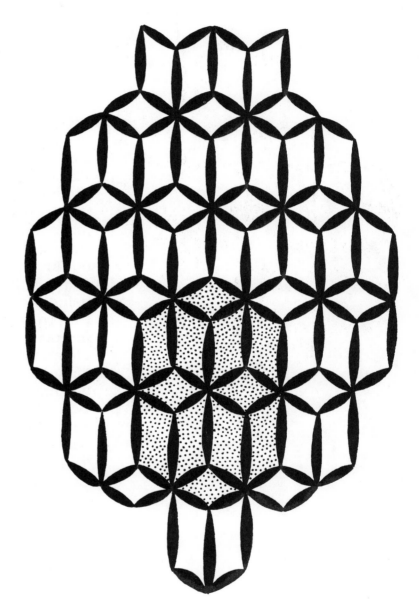

Shown on the right is the Cathedral Arcade grid. The
pattern of the hanging is defined by the shaded area. A
design of baby blocks might be possible.

Using Pattern Pieces

The following notes are a guide to the pattern pieces on the fold-out sheet at the center of the booklet. Each major pattern piece is shown half size. To make a full-size template to use when cutting fabric, you will need:

Materials:

Large sheets of wrapping paper (or gift wrap)
Pencil
Ruler
Paper cutting knife or scissors

Directions:

(1) Cut out a pattern piece.
(2) Place on a large sheet of folded wrapping paper matching "Place on Fold" edge with fold of wrapping paper.
(3) Trace around edge of pattern using ruler. Draw from tick mark to tick mark, taking care not to enlarge the outline.
(4) Cut out the template. Protect the cutting surface if using the paper cutting knife.
(5) Record notes from pattern piece onto unfolded template. Place tick marks as a guide to changing direction when tracing on or cutting fabric.
(6) Make a plastic template from the paper template when starting a large project such as a quilt.
(7) Window patterns must be given special handling. Set them aside until two finished units of the background grid have been joined, then see page 20, "Windows".
(8) Choosing the best patterns and colors for the window fabric is more important than following the grain line when cutting the fabric.

Cutting

Templates and Fabric

For your project choose a small Cathedral Spire pattern. The templates should be drawn and cut without seam allowances. When placing templates on fabric, remove one from the other by enough distance to allow for 1/4" seam allowance on the background pieces. A seam allowance should not be added to the window. The following instructions will produce the most accurate outline for any of the new Cathedral patterns. An adequate outline may be achieved by drawing around the template with the aid of a ruler.

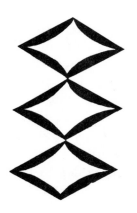

Materials:
Templates
Scissors
Pencils
Fabric markers
Needle and thread
Sandpaper board
Weights
Ruler

Directions:
1. Place fabric wrong side up (use sandpaper board for windows).
2. Place template on fabric. Locate and mark the center with a tailor tack, and leave it in place until unit is completed.
3. Replace template on fabric, matching centers, and observing grain line. Distribute weights over entire surface of template.
4. Use a fabric marker or pencil and place a small dot on the fabric at the edge of the template at the precise point that the line changes direction.
5. Connect the dots, using a ruler and referring back to the template each time you begin a new line.
6. Outline the number of pieces you need, leaving enough space between pieces for 1/4" seam allowances.
7. Cut out background pieces with 1/4" seam allowances; cut windows without seam allowances.

Windows

No two individuals install their windows in the same way. The framing of the windows makes the difference. They may be wide or narrow, flat or raised. Whatever the choice, the windows must be custom cut.

All windows must have:
(1) Points long enough to reach into the corners, but not beyond.
(2) Edges that will not bunch under the bias frame or break loose after being appliqued.

When two background units are sewn together you can decide how you are going to proceed. First, find the window that matches your pattern. Cut out a trial window from fabric scraps. Pin in place over the whipped seam. Turn the four bias edges over the window and pin. These edges create a frame for your window. You must choose; will it be wide or narrow?

A narrow frame will: lay flat against the grid, require a larger window, be easier to install and reveal more of the window fabric and less of the grid.

A wide frame will: create more tension above the grid, require a smaller window with sharply curved sides, take more careful pinning and coaxing to install and reveal more of the grid pattern and less of the window.

All window patterns must be cut to fit into the area of the window frame.

If the printed patterns do not meet your needs, refer to the section on pattern drafting.

Energy Saving Tips

Placing low-loft batting within each unit and behind each window creates as warm a quilt as anyone could desire. It remains a totally portable project that is finished unit by unit.

Detailed diagrams or directions are not necessary. Cathedral patterns can be "stuffed" after the first seams are sewn and the unit is turned right side out. Insert the batting and work it into position before closing the seam. Cut the batting to fit within the area defined by the broken lines in the illustrations. (For Cathedral Window, see illustration 6; for Cathedral Spire, see illustration 6; for Cathedral Gothic, see illustration 5; for Cathedral Arcade, see illustration 5.)

When the batting is cut to fit, roll it up, push it through the opening and work it into position with the blunt end of the crochet hook. Sew the opening shut and at the same time allow the stitches to catch the batting. Before folding the points to the center (the next step), run a few basting stitches where they won't be seen. This step and sewing the folded points in place will be enough tacking to hold the batting in place.

Stuffing the windows is even easier. A piece of batting is cut a little smaller than the window. Both batting and window are put in place at the same time; appliqueing the window in place serves to secure the batting.

The Well-Framed Window

Well-framed windows are the mark of the true craftsman (that could be a line in a building manual). Actually you would do well to approach each of the Cathedral patterns as construction projects. Their assembly is less like a pieced quilt and more like clothing construction.

(1) Bring out the sandpaper board. Lay the window fabric wrong side up on the rough surface. Place the template on the fabric. Grain line matters less than the pattern of the fabric. Pick the best spot and trace around the template with a sharp, soft, lead pencil.

(2) Cut out a single window. You may wish to make some minor alterations, and the template would then have to be trimmed. You will know if they are needed when you begin sewing.

(3) Optional: Cut a piece of low-loft batting conforming to the window in shape but slightly smaller all around.

(4) Place both window and batting over the whipped seam. Pin at the points. Insert the pins (aimed at the points) and leave them in place while you applique. The window should be fairly taut which may require trimming; adjust the template if you trim the window.

(5) Turn the bias over the window on all four sides. Watch those curves!

(6) Hide knots and tails of thread inside the window assembly. Take one stitch and give a tiny tug on the thread. Aim your needle carefully so that each stitch is reduced to a tiny dot along the edge of the bias frame.

(7) Three alternatives are shown for finishing the longer points. You have less choice on the shorter points because the edges barely meet, with coaxing.

All window patterns must be cut to fit into the area of the window frame.

If the printed patterns do not meet your needs refer to the section on pattern drafting.

1.

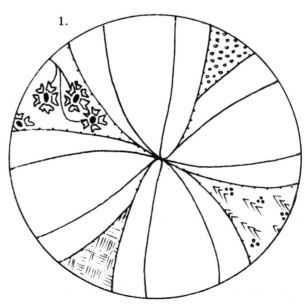

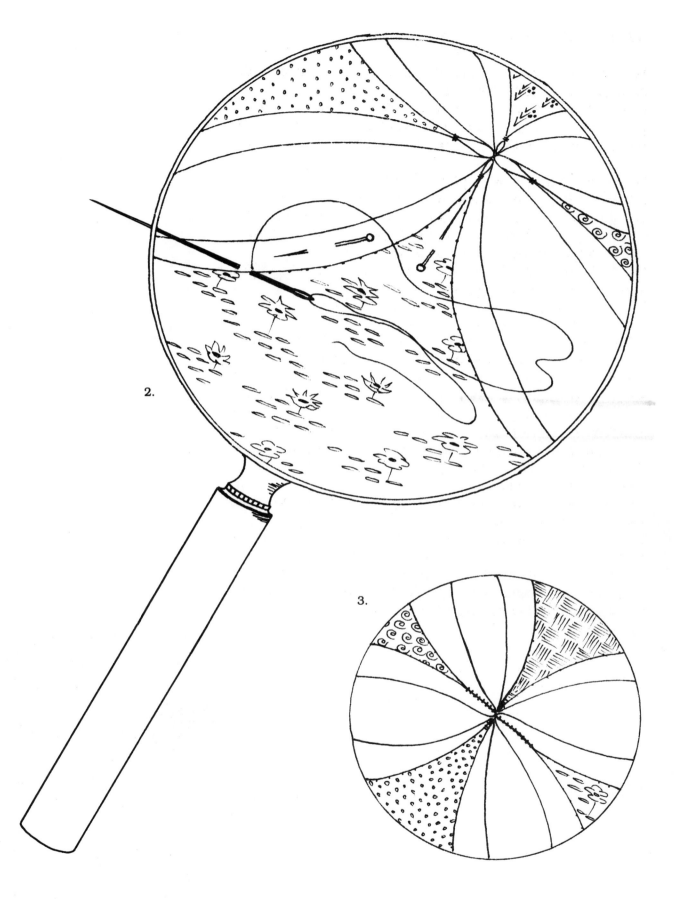

2.

3.

Three details for finishing the intersections

23

1.

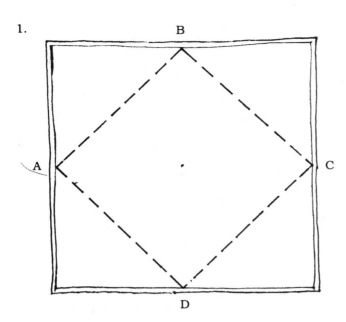

2.

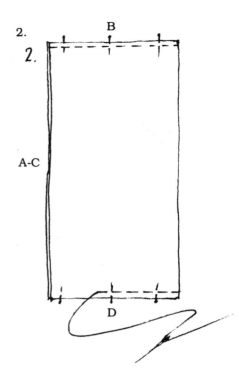

Cathedral Window

Sewing Instructions:
(1) Diagram shows cut pattern of square with fold lines (broken) and seam allowances.

(2) Fold square in half matching edge "A" to "C". Pin edges together matching seam allowance lines drawn on front and back. Seam by hand or machine.

(3) Refold and bring together edges "C" to "C" and "A" to "A".

(4) Pin edges, abutting seams at center. Sew across center to left edge. Sew from right edge toward center, leaving a small opening. Clip thread ends close to stitching.

3.

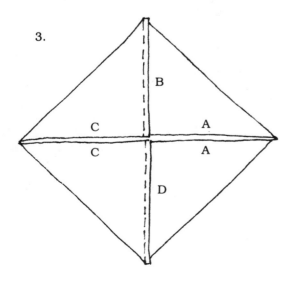

4.

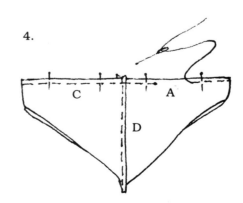

5.

6.

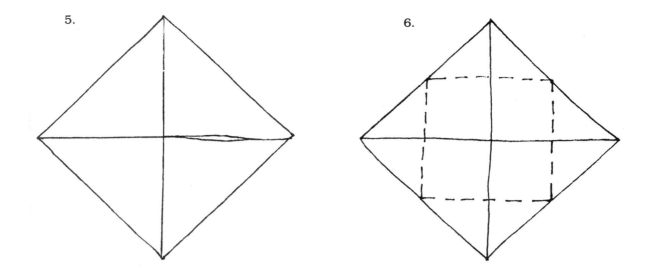

(5) Turn diamond right side out. Point out corners with blunt end of crochet hook. Flatten seams and pin or press. Sew opening shut. This step creates a "sealed" envelope of double thickness.

(6) Lay flat, seams up. Fold all four points of the square to center.

(7) Tack points together at center and through to the back of the square. Bring bias folds together at corners and secure with pins or temporary tacking. Pressing is optional. Make another square exactly like the first.

(8) Pin two finished squares together, back to back. Whip stitch together with fine stitches to withstand stress. Hide knots and tails of thread.

(9) Open and lay flat for window inset. This completes the background grid. Pressing of whip stitched seam is optional.

Note: Read all references concerning windows, "Windows", "Energy Saving Tips", "The Well Framed Window", "The Don'ts", "Window Patterns", and "Mounting the Template". See Table of Contents.

7.

8.

9.

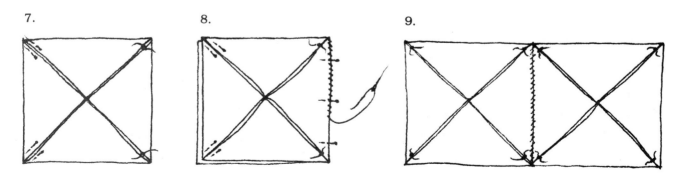

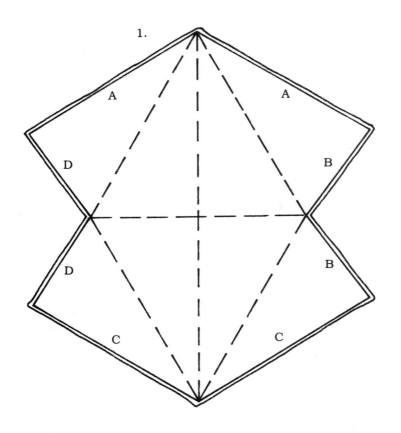

1.

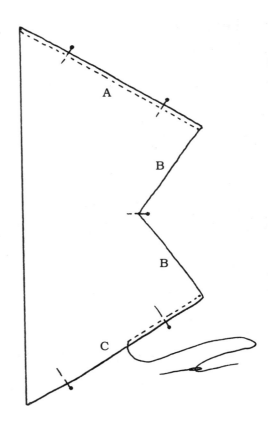

2.

Cathedral Spire

Sewing Instructions

(1) Diagram shows cut pattern of polygon with fold lines (broken) and seam allowances.

(2) Fold polygon in half matching edges "A" to "A" and "C" to "C". Pin edges together matching seam allowance lines drawn on front and back. Seam by hand or machine.

(3) Refold and bring together edges "D" to "D" and "B" to "B".

(4) Pin edges, abutting seams at center. Sew across center to left edge. Sew from right edge toward center, leaving a small opening. Clip thread ends close to stitching.

(5) Turn diamond right side out. Point out corners with blunt end of crochet hook. Flatten seams and pin or press. Sew opening shut. This step creates a "sealed" envelope of double thickness.

(6) Lay flat, seams up. Fold all four points of diamond to center.

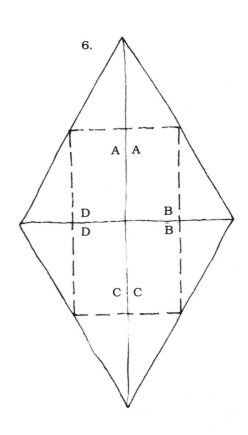

6.

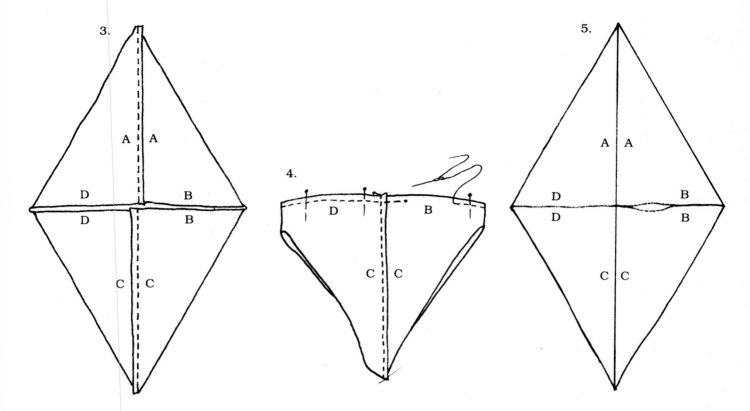

(7) Tack points together and through to the back of the rectangle. Bring bias folds at the four corners of the rectangle to sharp points. Secure with pins or temporary tacking. Pressing is optional. Make another rectangle exactly like the first.

(8) Pin two finished rectangles together, back to back. Whip stitch together with fine stitches to withstand stress. Hide knots and tails of thread.

(9) Open and lay flat for window inset. This completes the background "structure." Pressing of whip stitched seam is optional.

Note: Read all references concerning windows: "Windows," "Energy Saving Tips," "The Well Framed Window," The "Don'ts", "Window Patterns", and "Mounting the Template". See Table of Contents.

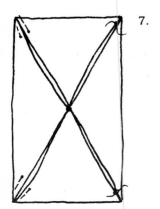

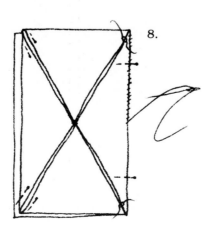

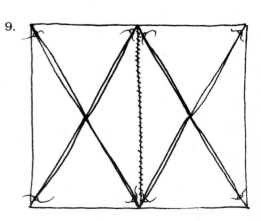

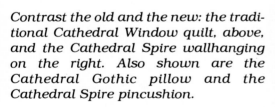

Contrast the old and the new: the traditional Cathedral Window quilt, above, and the Cathedral Spire wallhanging on the right. Also shown are the Cathedral Gothic pillow and the Cathedral Spire pincushion.

Photo by Cara Moore

28

The same Cathedral Arcade pattern was used for both the wallhanging, above right, and the table runner, below right. Two traditional Cathedral Window hangings appear on the left. Janet Kaiser's "Rose Window", above, mixes black and solid colors in the background and windows. "Acidita", below, is one of four arrangements possible from Rita Ericson's four-sectioned wallhanging, "Astral Series".

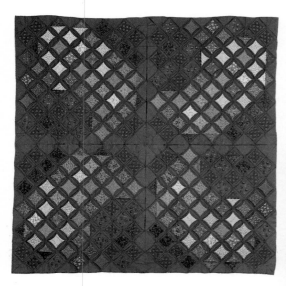

29

Sachet or Pincushion

Finished size: 3" x 5"

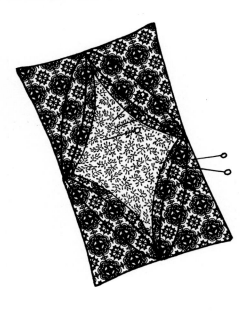

Wallhanging

Finished size: 12" x 37 1/2"

Materials:
12" x 20" rectangle of fabric for background units
6" x 7" rectangle of fabric for windows

Directions:
(1) Complete two units made from Cathedral Spire #1 pattern. Following through from step #9 of the "Sewing Instructions" and the installation of one window produces two attached units. Fold these two units back to back. Pin and whip stitch the long edges together.
(2) Applique another window into the frame created by the new whip stitched seam.
(3) Turn inside out so that the windows face each other precisely. Pin in place and whip stitch one end closed.
(4) Turn right side out. Fill with your choice of stuffing, if it is to be a pincushion. For a sachet, choose one of the following: dried lavender, spice tea (known by several different regional names), your own herb mixture or whole cloves.
(5) Blind stitch end to close.

Materials:
2 1/4 yds. of 45" fabric for background units
1/2 yd. of 45" fabric for windows (less if pattern matching is unimportant)
13" rod or wooden dowel
Optional: tassels

Directions:
This project makes a very attractive hanging with a minimum of work after the windows are installed. If you buy tassels, literally nothing has to be done, except to sew them on the wallhanging and then slip the rod through the folds in the top three units.

(1) Follow "Cathedral Spire Sewing Instructions" use Cathedral Spire #3 pattern.
(2) Assemble the bottom three units first. Only three of the four points are folded to the center and tacked in place.
(3) One need not be limited to nine units. Six units would be the minimum; however, size is limited only by time and enthusiasm. Perhaps you have a wall above a couch or bookcase that needs a horizontal accent. Visualize the hanging turned sideways with the wide points untacked at the bottom. (The rod would have to be longer.) With more numerous units in the completed wallhanging, the windows could be varied in tone from dark to light creating a pleasing visual effect.

Materials:
36 yds. of 45" fabric for background grid
4 yds. of 45" fabric for windows
4 yds. of low-loft batting for windows is optional

Directions:
The materials given are adequate for a double-bed quilt. A total of 233 units make the pillow panel and a quilt large enough to cover a standard mattress. This size will require a dust ruffle on the box spring. For a pleasing, custom effect consider making the dust ruffle from the same fabric used for the windows.

The quilt is made of 165 units each measuring 5" x 7". Assemble them with 15 units across the top of the bed making the 75" width and 11 units, end to end, for the 77" length. The panel for covering two standard pillows is 4 units wide and 17 units long. This creates a heavy quilt so consider a lightweight fabric of mixed fabric content. Inquire about discounts when buying yardage by the bolt. Thirty-four yards of 45" fabric will make the required number of units if the fabric is cut very carefully without waste. Two yards have been added for human error (or a pillow).

(1) Prewash all fabric. A 50-50 or 60-40 fabric mix will have the additional advantage of requiring very little pressing.
(2) After washing, cut the fabric in 31" x 45" rectangles. Six units may be cut from each rectangle. Remember the seam allowances.
(3) For assembly of each unit, see pages 26-27 and follow "Cathedral Spire Sewing Instructions."

Quilt

Finished size: 75" x 77"

Pillow cover: 28" x 85"

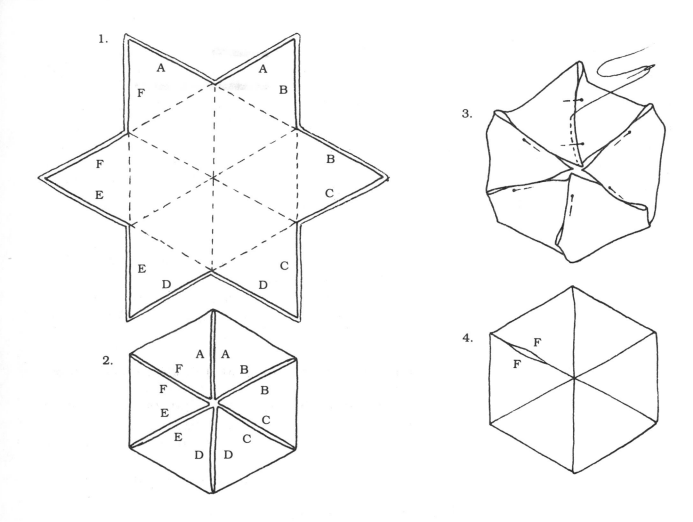

Cathedral Gothic

Sewing Instructions

To get a feel for the pattern, as few as two units may be sewn together. The following instructions assume that you will choose to make an assembly of six units. Cathedral Gothic #1 was used for the pillow. Cathedral Gothic #2 was used for the red poinsettia.

(1) Diagram shows cut pattern of six-pointed star.
(.2) Fold points of the star to the center.
(3) Pin together each pair of adjacent edges beginning with "A" to "A". Pin through the two layers of cloth, point to point, keeping the seam allowances in alignment, front to back. Start each seam at the points and work toward the outer edge. Leave a 2" opening in the middle of the last seam.
(4) Turn right side out. Point out corners with blunt end of crochet hook. Turn all seams in one direction and finger press or iron. Sew opening shut.

5.

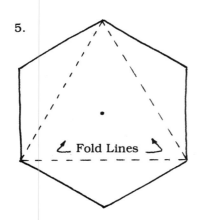

Fold Lines

6.

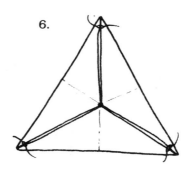

7.

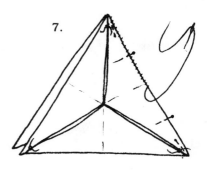

(5) Lay flat, seams face down. Fold alternate points of the hexagon to the center.

(6) Tack center points together and through to the back of the triangle. Bring bias edges together in a sharp point at all three corners of the triangle. Pin or secure with a small, tight tailor tack (to be removed later).

(7) Pin together two finished triangles, back to back, matching ends. Whip stitch together along one edge, by hand. Place fine stitches close together to withstand stress. Hide knots and tails of thread.

(8) Add a third triangle. Assemble the remaining three triangles.

(9) Connect the two halves of the hexagon. Pin together, back to back, matching centers and ends. Whip stitch as in step #7.

(10) The enlarged detail of the window assembly can be completed after reading all references about window installations listed in the Table of Contents. Included are: "Windows", "Energy Saving Tips", "The Well Framed Window", "The "Don'ts", "Window Patterns", and "Mounting the Template".

8.

9.

9.

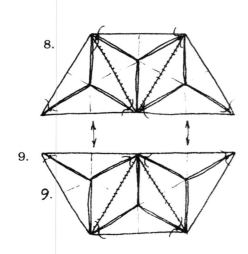

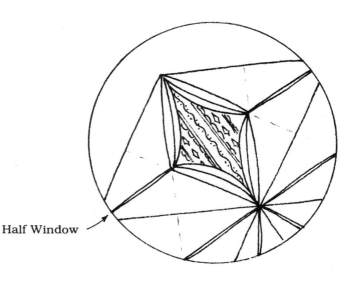

Half Window

Pillow

Finished size: 15" hexagon

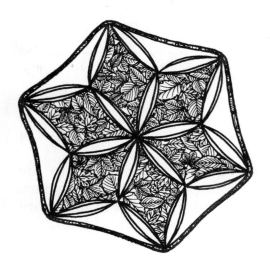

Materials:

1 yd. of 45" fabric for background units and 6 half-windows

1/2 yd. of 45" fabric for pillow backing, windows and cording cover

60" of 1/4" cording

14" zipper

8" x 30" low-loft polyester batting for window backing

Directions:

(1) Complete 6 units of Cathedral Gothic #1 pattern and install windows, following the 10 steps of "Cathedral Gothic Sewing Instructions".

(2) Cut 6 half-windows using Cathedral Gothic window #1 pattern.

(3) Install half-windows on outside edge of hexagon turning bias edges over windows on the two curved sides. (See step 10, "Sewing Instructions".)

(4) Fold straight edge of each half-window to the wrong side of pillow. Secure with careful basting.

(5) Cover 60" of cording with 60" of 1 7/8"-wide continuous bias. (See Table of Contents, "Continuous Bias".)

(6) Beginning about 2" back from one end, pin cording to pillow edge. Place first pin at approximate center of one side of hexagon. Leave ends free to be telescoped at finish. Ease cording at corners.

(7) Blind stitch cording to pillow face keeping right side toward you. Keep edge of pillow snug against cording so that stitch line is covered. End stitching about 3" from beginning.

(8) Prepare ends of covered cording to telescope by peeling the bias back to reveal the cord ends. Allow the ends to overlap and nestle in against the pillow edge. Cut through the two pieces of cording so as to leave abutting ends.

(9) Extend the sleeve of bias over the cording on one end and trim bias even with the cording. On the other end leave 1" of bias extending beyond the end of the cording. Turn back a narrow hem on this end and press.

(10) Telescope the two ends by working the cut off end into the open sleeve of bias until the two ends of cording meet. They should lie flat against the pillow edge.

(11) Repair the cording at the joining and catch the narrow hem of the sleeve with several fine stitches.

(12) Blind stitch the free section of cording to the pillow.

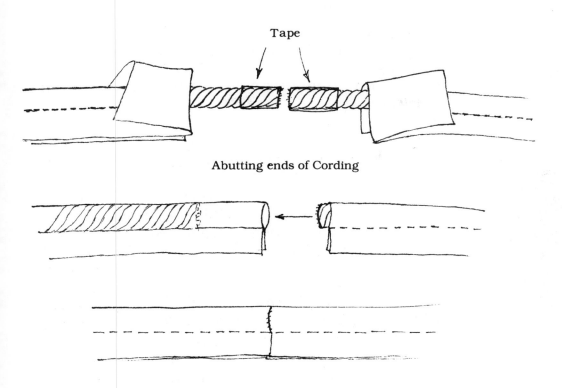

Tape

Abutting ends of Cording

Pillow Form

Materials:
1/2 yd. of high-loft, coarse, polyester batting for cover
1 small bag of polyester pillow filling to stuff form
  (scraps of batting may be pulled apart and substituted)

Directions:
(1) Cut two hexagons the same size as the pillow from the batting.
(2) Place face to face and stitch around 1/2" in from outside edge, leaving one side open between stitched corners. Do not turn right side out.
(3) Fill with polyester filling (or scraps).
(4) Sew opening shut by hand or machine.
(5) Place pillow form in pillow and work corners into position.

If bulges appear on half-windows on pillow face, tuck and pin the extra fabric to preserve desired contours. A few well placed stitches will catch and hold the fabric in place. The problem will be most obvious at corners of the hexagon.

Pillow Backing and Zipper:

(1) Cut two pieces measuring 10" x 18" from the 1/2 yd. of 45" fabric.

(2) Turn back and press a 3/4" hem on the 18" edge of each piece.

(3) Place zipper, right side up, between the two 18" edges. Stitch in zipper. Seam fabric together at both ends of zipper.

(4) Place pillow backing face down. Using front of pillow as a template, cut the backing into a hexagon making it 1" larger all around. Zipper should bisect hexagon corner to corner.

(5) Remove backing of pillow to ironing board, face down. Turn and press a 1" hem around edge of hexagon, mitering corners.

(6) With wrong sides together, pin backing to face of pillow, easing in fullness and matching corners. Nestle the backing into the "ditch" along the stitch line of the cording and blind stitch all around the edge.

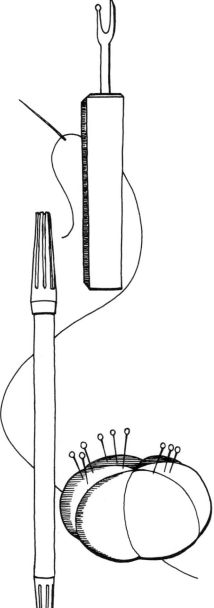

4.
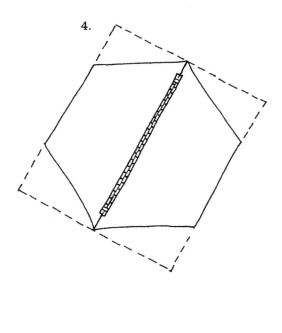

Poinsettia Basket Cover

The poinsettia will cover Christmas candies placed in a 6" to 8" diameter basket and make a charming gift.

Finished size: 10 1/4" x 10 1/4"

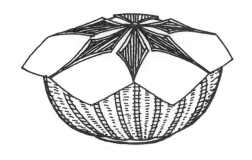

Materials:
2/3 yd. of 45" fabric for background units
9" x 12" piece of fabric for windows
Button or ring for center of finished poinsettia

Directions:
(1) Complete 6 units of Cathedral Gothic #2 pattern following "Cathedral Gothic Sewing Instructions" through step #5.
(2) Tack center points together but not permanently and not through to the back of the triangle; tacking will be removed later.
(3) Make 5 more triangles exactly like the first.
(4) Continue on with "Cathedral Gothic Sewing Instructions" resuming with step #7, however be sure to install windows without batting.
(5) When all windows are installed cut the loose tacking at centers of each triangle. This should release all points of each unit.
(6) Press flat the outside points of the enlarged hexagon. Pinch together the side points of each window installation and press.
(7) Sew on button or ring at center of hexagon.

37

Cathedral Arcade

Sewing Instructions

Finished size: 24" x 36" (outside dimensions with irregular contours)

Materials:

2 1/2 yds. of 45" fabric for background units
1/3 yd. each of two different fabrics for windows
Optional: 30" x 30" thin or traditional batting

The assembly consists of 12 units cut from the large Cathedral Arcade pattern. All units should be assembled in the same way through step #4.

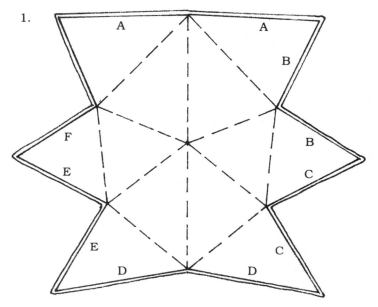

Directions:

(1) The pattern outline with seam allowances.
(2) Fold points to the center bringing together all raw edges of the pattern.

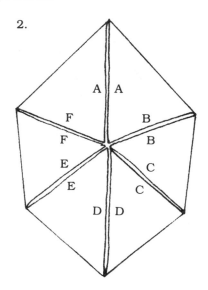

3.

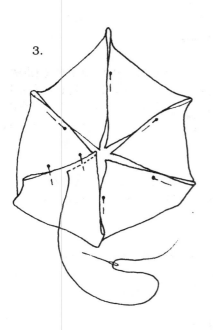

(3) Pin together each pair of adjacent edges. Start each seam at the points in the center and work toward the outer edge. This step requires precision. Point must match point, front and back. The seam in front must line up with the seam in back. Leave a 2" opening in the middle of one seam for turning.

4.

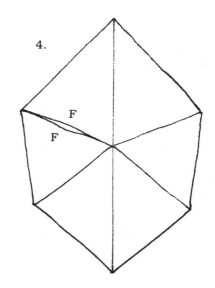

(4) Turn the polygon right side out. Point out the corners using blunt end of the crochet hook. Press seams in a spiral. Take a couple of stitches to close any gap or hole at the center. Sew opening shut. Finish 11 more units (step 1 through 4) and set aside.

5.

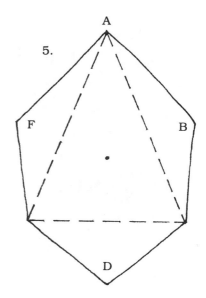

(5) Lay one finished unit flat with seams face down. Be sure that point "A" is at the top and point "D" at the bottom. Beginning with point "D", fold alternate points to the center. This brings "F-B-D" to the center.

6.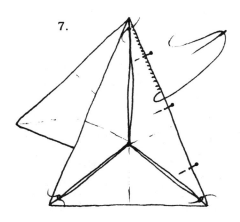

7.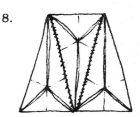

8.

9.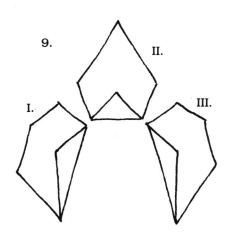

I.   II.   III.

10. & 11.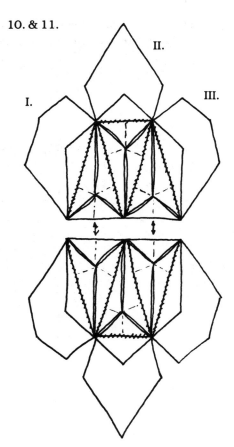

II.

I.   III.

(6) Tack "F-B-D" at the center and through to the back of the triangle. Pin or tack the bias folds together at the corners. Pressing is optional. Finish 5 more units in the same way.

(7) Pin together two finished triangles, back to back, matching ends. Note position of the back triangle in the diagram. The peak (point "A") of the back triangle should be matched with the lower right corner of the triangle in front. Whip stitch together along one edge placing stitches close together to withstand stress. Hide knots and tails of thread.

(8) Add a third triangle. Make another set of three triangles.

(9) Of the six remaining units, make two each to match I, II, III, in the following manner.
Fold "D" up to the center mark on 2 units, tack lightly.
Fold "F" up to the center mark on 2 units, tack lightly.
Fold "B" up to the center mark on 2 units, tack lightly.
Optional: To insert batting, open a seam about 2" on the back. Cut and place batting in each of the six units and close seams.

(10) Arrange the finished units to conform to diagram. Pair off, two units at a time, back to back. Whip stitch the six seams.

(11) Join the two halves of the assembly with one whip stitched seam, matching and pinning centers and ends.

(12) Open and lay flat. Pressing of whip stitched seams is optional.

Note: Read all references concerning windows, "Windows", "Energy Saving Tips", "The Well Framed Window", The "Don'ts", "Window Patterns", and "Mounting the Template". See Table of Contents.

Bias Border for Wallhanging

Two-inch-wide bias was cut from a square of fabric 20" x 20". Follow the directions for "Continuous Bias" (see Contents) drawing the guide lines 2" apart in step 3. When cut the completed "sleeve" will make 188" of bias 2" wide. This is adequate bias to frame the Cathedral Arcade design in the border pattern shown in the photo. The bias was pressed to the width of 1" using a template cut from a shirt cardboard. Cut the template 1" x 8" and move along the center of the 2" strip of bias, ironing the edges toward the center all the way. Pin the pressed bias in place following the contours of the pattern and the edge of the background. Pleat the bias at each turn and hide the pleated fabric on the wrong side of the strip. The strip was sewn in place by hand using blind stitch hemming on both sides of the bias.

Table Runner

Finished size: 15 1/4"x35"

Materials:

1 2/3 yd. of 45" fabric for the background units
Minimum of 1/2 yd. of 45" fabric for the windows and
   much more if a pattern is used
1/2 yd. batting

Directions:

1. Complete 8 units of the Cathedral Arcade pattern. Assemble the 8 units in the shape of a diamond. Install 8 windows and the piece is finished.
2. A fabric button may be appliqued over the center intersection of seams as pictured.

Wallhanging

Finished size: 33" x 44"

Materials:

Completed assembly of 12 units of Cathedral Arcade pattern.

33" of nonwoven interfacing to back the finished wall-hanging

1 1/4 yds. of 45" fabric backing and loops for mounting 12 unit assembly

Optional: 30" x 30" thin or traditional batting

Directions:

The wallhanging consists of 12 units cut from Cathedral Arcade pattern and assembled, following "Cathedral Arcade Sewing Instructions". When the assembly of the pattern is complete, prepare the backing.

(1) Cut 1 yd. from the 1 1/4 yds. of fabric for backing. Turn and press hems on either side to 33" width. (45" fabric will shrink to approximately 44", the length of the mounted pattern.)

(2) Trim nonwoven interfacing to within 1/4" of the backing material.

(3) Make a tube of the remaining fabric and stitch the length of the tube 1 1/2" wide. (The width is optional but it should be kept in proportion to the size of the rod.) Turn right side out and press.

(4) Wrap the tube around the rod, and allowing for another 1 1/2" to 2" for sewing, trim off first loop.

(5) Cut as many additional loops as desired.

(6) Fold all loops in half and press.

(7) Insert raw edges of loops between nonwoven interfacing and backing material along top edge of backing. Arrange in even spacing across top edge, pin in place and test to be sure the rod has adequate space to pass through loop.

(8) Measure and pin all loops in place. Continue pinning around all edges of backing to hold nonwoven interfacing and backing material flat and uniform.

(9) Determine minimal distance for stitching close to edge then stitch all around outside edge of backing to secure nonwoven interfacing, backing material and loops.

(10) Center Cathedral Arcade assembly on backing material and pin in place. Tack to backing at points.

Optional: Quilt the pattern of a two sided triangle on the six protruding flaps of the assembly.

**Batting Patterns
for Wallhanging**

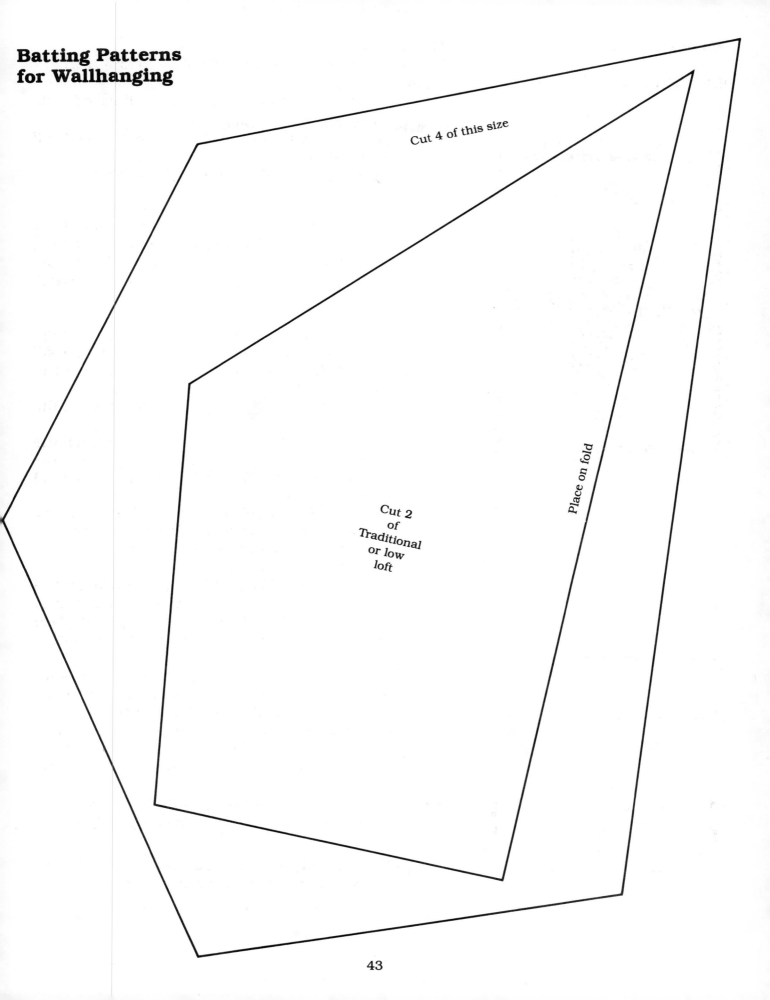

Cut 4 of this size

Place on fold

Cut 2
of
Traditional
or low
loft

Continuous Bias

(1) Cut a piece of fabric 11" square on the grainline. Draw a diagonal line connecting two corners.

(2) Cut along the diagonal line and rejoin with a 1/4" seam. Press the seam open.

(3) Draw three lines parallel to the top and bottom edges approximately 1 7/8" apart.

(4) Form a tube or sleeve with right sides matching, and lines staggered. (Line "1" joins line "2", "2" joins "3", "3" joins "4", and "4" goes off in space.) Pin and stitch a 1/4" seam. Press seam open.

Begin cutting along the free top section. Continue cutting in a spiral to the end.

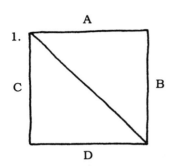

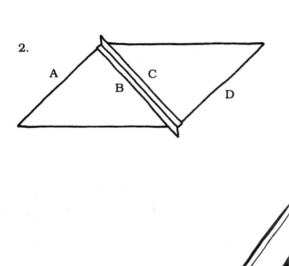

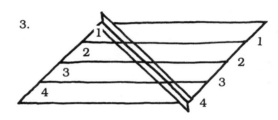

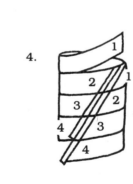

An 11" square of fabric will make 60" of 1 7/8" bias.

A 12" square of fabric will make about 66" of 2" bias.

The progression is rapid as the size of the square is increased. For quilt binding, note:

36" square will make 13 yds. of 2 1/2" bias binding.
43" square will make 20 yds. of 2 1/2" bias binding.

Pattern Drafting

The following pages contain instructions for creating a custom pattern of any size, for any of the three new designs: Cathedral Spire, Cathedral Gothic and Cathedral Arcade.

This may be unfamiliar territory and a little intimidating. Take heart! You can't go faster than one step at a time and that leads, inevitably to a finished drawing, creating a pattern to fill your special need.

General Instructions

If a project requires a pattern of a size different from those presented in the center tear-out section, help is at hand. With these instructions you can draft your own pattern. The size you want may deviate as little as half an inch; however, it is the subtle change in the angle of a line that is so important to a good assembly. *(No short cuts are possible.)* A new pattern must be drafted.

The drawings in this section are intended for reference only; however, a template can be made from a tracing of any of the patterns.

Materials:
Ruler
Compass
Eraser
Pencils - soft lead
Paper - large sheets
Scissors

Directions:
(1) Refer to the pattern throughout your drawing.
(2) Draw all construction lines lightly; make pattern lines heavier.
(3) When two arcs have been drawn, mark the precise point of intersection with a small dot.
(4) A ruler may be substituted for a compass, and it may be necessary for a larger pattern. Consider the corner of the ruler as the point of the compass. Pivot the ruler on this imaginary compass "trip" and make arcs with a series of dots as you progress.
(5) When you have finished drafting the pattern, test for accuracy. Cut out the template. Fold all points to the center (four on Cathedral Spire, six on Cathedral Gothic and Cathedral Arcade). The cut edges should meet but not gap or overlap. Minor adjustments can be made without redrafting.
(6) When you are satisfied that you have an accurate template, label it with: the pattern name, finished size of rectangle or triangle, grain line, note about 1/4" seam allowance, tick marks at all points.

Cathedral Spire

(1) Determine the dimensions of the rectangle you wish to draft.

(2) Draw a line horizontally through the center of the paper. Find the approximate center of the line. Label it "G". All measurements will be made from "G". Open compass to the width of your rectangle. With compass at "G" draw an arc to the left of "G" and one to the right. Both arcs should intersect the horizontal line. Label these points "H" and "I".

(3) Open compass from "H" to "I". With compass on "H", draw two arcs, one in line with and below "G", the other above and in line with "G". Move compass to "I" and do the same. Connect these two points through "G" and extend them above and below the intersection of the arcs.

(4) Open compass to the length of the rectangle. With point on "G", draw an arc on the vertical line above "G" and one below "G". Label these points "J" and "K".

(5) Open the compass from "G" to "H". With the point on "H", draw a wide arc above "H", another below. Move compass to "I". Draw an arc above "I", another below.

(6) Open compass from "G" to "J". With point at "J", intersect arc above "H" and above "I". Label these two points "L" and "M".

(7) Move point of compass to "K" with same setting. Intersect the arcs below "H" and "I". Label these points "N" and "O".

(8) With ruler, connect all points around outline of pattern. This forms a polygon.

(9) Draw a broken line connecting "H-J-I-K". This line should intersect the wide arcs above and below "H" and "I". These points are the corners of your rectangle. Connect them to complete the drafting of your pattern.

(10) Label the completed pattern with notes about: name of pattern, size of rectangle, 1/4" seam allowance, fold lines (broken lines), grain of fabric.

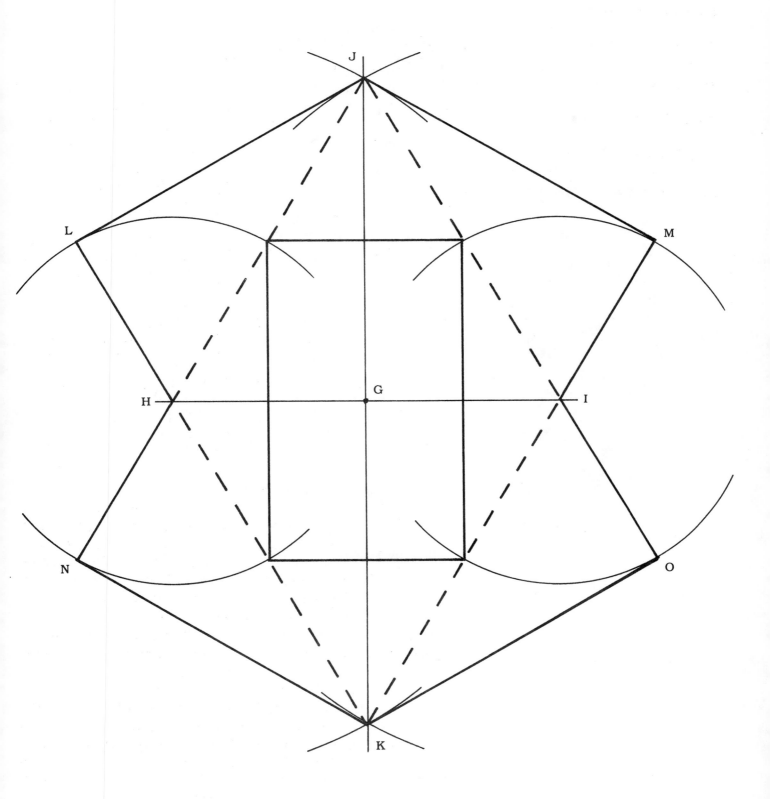

(1) Determine the size of your finished triangle. Measure one side (all sides must be equal). Draw a line the same length near center of paper. Label ends of line "H" and "I".

(2) Open compass from "H" to "I". With compass at "H", draw an arc above base line "H-I". Move compass to "I" and draw an intersecting arc. Label the crossing of lines "J". Connect "H-I-J". This is your equilateral triangle.

(3) Find the center points on "H-I", "I-J" and "J-H".

(4) Draw a light line from:
•point "J" through center point on "H-I" and beyond
•point "I" through center point on "H-J" and beyond
•point "H" through center point on "I-J" and beyond.
These lines should cross precisely at the center of the triangle. Label the center point "G". All measurements are taken from center point "G".

(5) Open compass from "G" to "H". Draw a complete circle with point at "G". It should touch all three points of the triangle. It should intersect all three lines drawn through the triangle. Label the new points "K-L-M".

(6) Connect points "H-L-J-M-I-K-H" with a broken line. This makes a hexagon. Repeat the next two steps six times around the hexagon. And behold a star is born!

(7) Open compass from "G" to "H". With compass on "H", draw an arc outside the circle between "H" and "K", another between "H" and "L". Move compass around from "H" to "L" to "J" to "M" to "I" to "K", making arcs from each point until there are six pairs of intersecting arcs. Label these points "N", "O", "P", "Q", "R", and "S".

(8) "N-H-K-R" should form a straight line. Line up the ruler with all four points. Draw star points in solid lines. Repeat this step around the six sides of the hexagon until the star outline is complete.

(9) Label the pattern with notes about: name of pattern, size of triangle, 1/4" seam allowance, fold lines (broken lines), grain of fabric.

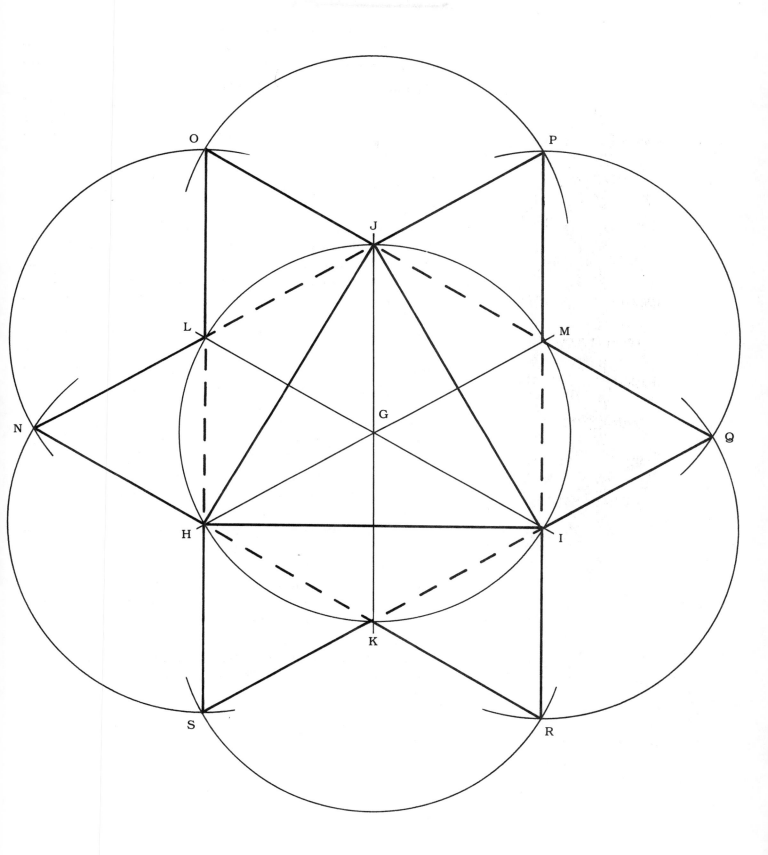

(1) Determine the size of your triangle. It must have a base line shorter than its sides. The sides will be equal to one another in length. Draw the base line and label it "H-I".

(2) Open compass from "H" to "I". With point at "H" draw arcs centered above and below "H-I"; move compass to "I" and do the same. Draw line connecting intersecting points and extend line well above base line toward "K" on diagram. Label point "J" on base line.

(3) Measure height of your triangle, base to top. Transfer this measurement to your drawing starting at "J". Label the new point "K". Connect points "H-K-I". This creates your isosceles triangle.

(4) "G" is an arbitrary point along line "J-K" that determines the shape of your windows. Mark this point about one-third to half the way up from base line "H-J-I". Label this point "G". All compass measurements will be made from "G" which is the center of your pattern.

(5) Open compass from "G" to "J". With point on "J", draw an arc on line below "J". Label this point "L".

(6) Open compass from "G" to "H". With point on "H", draw a half circle to the left of "H". Move compass to "I". Draw a half circle to the right of "I".

(7) Open compass from "G" to "L". With compass on "L", draw arcs to intersect the half circles on left and right of "L". Label these points "M" and "N".

(8) Open compass from "G" to "K". With compass on "K", draw two wide arcs. Each of these arcs must intersect the half circles on left and right and continue on an upswing to the level of "K". Label these points "O" and "P".

(9) Open compass from "G" to "O". With compass on "O", draw two arcs. One will intersect the line on the left and above "O", one to the left and below. Move the compass to "P" and draw two arcs to the right, above and below "P". Label these points "Q", "R", "S" and "T".

(10) Follow diagram and outline the polygon with a broken line, connecting points "K-P-I-L-H-O" and "K".

(11) Follow diagram and outline the pattern with a solid line connecting "K-S-P-T-I-N-L-M-H-Q-O-R" and back to "K".

(12) Label the pattern with notes about: name of pattern, size of triangle, 1/4" seam allowance, fold lines (broken lines), grain of fabric.

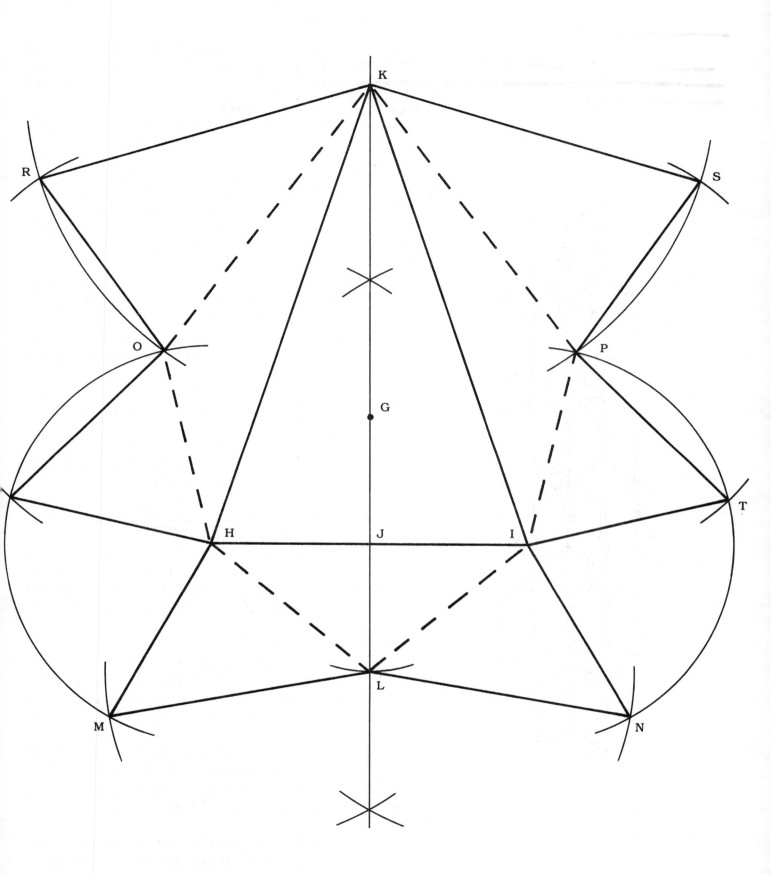

Cathedral Window:

A sheet of typing paper and scissors are all that one needs to make a template for the traditional Cathedral Window pattern. One *careful* fold and one cut produce a true square.

(1) Fold the paper so that "A" meets "B".
(2) Hold loosely and pinch a precise point at "C".
(3) Line up the edges "A-C" and "B-C" and continue the crease away from "C" along the fold line.
(4) Cut along "D-B"

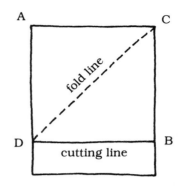

Standard typing paper measures 8 1/2"x11". Your template should measure 8 1/2" square and will make a finished unit 4" square. To create a template of a larger size, use a sheet of pre-cut gift wrap or a sheet from the daily newspaper. This simple formula can be your guide.

(1) Choose size of square (finished); example - 2 1/2" finished square.
(2) Double that size; example - 5" square.
(3) Add 1/2" (for seams 1/4" wide); example - 5 1/2" square.

A piece of fabric 6 1/2" square makes a 3" square finished unit.
A piece of fabric 8 1/2" square makes a 4" square finished unit.
A piece of fabric 10 1/2" square makes a 5" square finished unit.
A piece of fabric 12 1/2" square makes a 6" square finished unit.
A piece of fabric 14 1/2" square makes a 7" square finished unit.
A piece of fabric 16 1/2" square makes an 8" square finished unit.
A piece of fabric 18 1/2" square makes a 9" square finished unit.

My good New England heritage prompted me to always cut fabric with an eye to economy when I could. When I made the brown quilt shown in the color plates, I bought 45"-wide fabric for the background. After washing, I cut off the selvage which left me with 44"-wide fabric. I divided the 44" width into four equal strips 11" wide and cut the strips into squares as I needed them. Not a scrap was wasted!

Window Patterns

Materials:
Two completed units of any pattern
Paper, pencil and scissors

Directions:
(1) Fold paper in half.
(2) Place folded edge along the edge of the whip stitched seam.
(3) Lightly sketch a half diamond to conform to the uncovered side.
(4) Remove the paper to a hard surface. Redraw the lines, curving each line inward toward the fold in the paper. This curved line forms the outside edge of your window "frame".
(5) Fold the paper in half again, matching the end points of the diamond. Keep the best curve on top.
(6) Cut out the template.
(7) Unfold the template and place over the whip stitched seam at the center of the two joined units. The template should extend into the four points but not beyond. The bias edges of fabric should turn over the edges of the template without creating gaps or bunching.
(8) Make alterations in the template as needed. Even this altered template may require further alterations as you sew the first window in place.
(9) When the template has proven satisfactory it can be mounted on plastic.

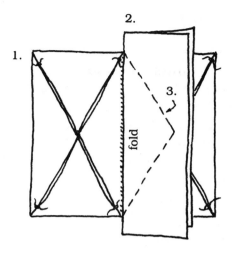

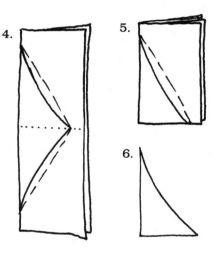

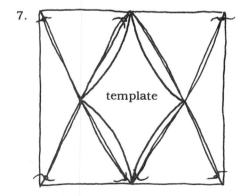

Mounting the Template

A large paper pattern may be used as a template without mounting. All window templates should be mounted.

Materials:
Glue stick or rubber cement
Scissors
Pencils

(1) Cut out the paper pattern but not on the outline. When possible leave a small margin of paper on the outside of the outline.
(2) Mount the pattern on plastic with stick glue or rubber cement.
(3) Allow time for the bonding agent to dry.
(4) Cut around the outline with care, but not with your best scissors. Cut as close to the edge as possible without nipping into the outline.
(5) Label the template with the name and size of the finished unit.

The following are the major pitfalls in making all Cathedral patterns. Always keep in mind that Cathedral patterns are "3-D" patterns, not flat. Much of their appeal depends on this unique characteristic of the design to keep them looking their perky best.

The "Don'ts"

(1) Avoid careless corners. Tailor tacks or pins will solve the problem. The cloth must be disciplined if it is to retain a precise geometric shape.

(2) Avoid loose windows. Refer to "The Well Framed Window", step 4, which indicates that the window should be "fairly taut". Pin and repin the window if necessary. But trim the tip of the window only when you are sure that you have excess fabric at the points. I wait until I am working with needle and thread before I trim the tip.

(3) Avoid windows that are too large. When they are cut just right they may look a little small. When the bias is folded over the raw edge of the window it should create a deep curve without bunching (or leaving gaps). A little tension in the window between curves of the bias is good.

(4) Avoid flat window installations. Failing to turn the bias as far it will go will show more of the window but very little of the grid pattern. Each one needs to be featured, the grid and the windows.

(5) Avoid windows that won't "open". When the window "installation" is complete you should be able to slip your hand underneath it. Fortunately it is easier to do it correctly than to "lock it shut". You will want to grasp your work by slipping your hand under the window assembly as you sew. Appliqueing becomes easier if you do. The needle should go through the window, the batting and the bias flap (on return), but not penetrate the last two layers of cloth that form the wrong side of the unit.

(6) Avoid loose or inadequate tacking. Points at the center of each unit should be tacked securely together and through to the wrong side of the unit. Floaters, not fastened to the wrong side, will cause the grid to shift. The second stress point is at each corner of the window assembly where bias meets bias.

(7) Avoid careless whip stitching. Catch all four layers of fabric in the needle at the beginning and end of each seam. Ease up, catching fewer layers in the middle. But watch the ends and beginnings. Failing this, the fabric will balloon out near the points during installation of the windows.